A GOD WHO SEES YOU

A GOD WHO SEES YOU

FAYE THOMAS

DEDICATION

I would like to dedicate this book to My Savior Jesus Christ first, then my Pastor, Walter N. Willis Jr, First Lady Kim Willis, and Laura Hylton for inspiriting me to write this book. Thank you from the bottom of my heart.

I also would like to dedicate this book to my husband, John Kennedy Thomas (Kenny), and my three children: Martigus Johnson, Kendrick Thomas, and Destini Thomas. And let not forget about my beautiful grandchildren: Shalayia Thomas, Jayla Johnson, Elani Burton, Israel Thomas, and Mia Henderson, I love them with all my might.

Also, Valarie Lumpkin, Herline Knights, and Dr. Beze Adogu for your encouraging words. Believing in me and telling me I can do it.

Faye one who tells you the truth with love rather it hurts or not. One that after talking with, you feel better, like you can make it! Encouraged!

Laura Hylton

Table of Contents

Introduction

Seeking God in this uncertain world, through the heartaches and pains. Anything can happen or has happened. Terrorist attacks, diseases, perilous times, and famine.

But during all this, the Lord's word says (Amos 8: 11) "Behold the days come, saith the Lord God, that I will send a famine in the land, not a famine of bread, nor a thirst for water, but of hearing the words of the Lord:"

All this negative news surrounding us now. Lord help us. My heart goes out to all the families that have lost a loved one or friend during this devastating time. But there is a way to get help. Psalm 121 says 1. I will lift up my eyes unto the hills, from whence cometh my help. 2. My help cometh from the Lord Who hath made heaven and earth.

I had to learn how to trust in my God. I could not make it without Him. Also, I want to acknowledge my Pastor, Walter N. Willis, Jr. Thank you for your guidance and direction during my darkest times. You help me to see and hear God when I thought I was all alone. Also, I want to thank my First Lady Kim Willis for the long talks, making me realize I have a voice and to keep it moving. My best friend Laura Hylton for always supporting me and being there when I needed a shoulder.

Most of all my husband John K. Thomas and the Children (Martigus Johnson, Kendrick Thomas, and Destini Thomas) for always saying pray for us and giving me all the support I need. Loving me and seeing God in me.

I want to encourage someone with this book to lean on Jesus when everyone around you is telling you **"no"** but Jesus is telling you "yes". Step out with faith and watch what He will do. But you must keep a clean heart and mind when trusting God, He is not involved in any negative vibe. I love you all, please pray for me, my family, and my church family, In Jesus Name.

CHAPTER ONE

If It Had Not Been for the Lord

Psalm 124:1-2

G od is calling His people right now. What has God done for you, has he been good to you. Can you praise Him, and acknowledge Him. Just thank Him. He is worthy. Put on a happy face and praise my God. Leave the negative out and praise Him. It does not matter what church folks have done to you, just see what God has done for you. I do not care how they look at you because His eyes are on the sparrow and you know He watches over you. I know what folks do to you, mistreat you, drag and scandalize your good name, lie on you, and look you over. Hit you in the front and stab you in the back. I might not be what I ought to be, but I thank God I am not what I used to be. If it had not been for the Lord. His mercy, peace, long-suffering, patience, love, grace, and guidance where would I be.

As you look out at everything that has happened now, black lives matter, hate crimes, COVID-19, etc., I for sure know God has a plan. It may seem like a disaster right now, but in a disaster is when God does the most. Your life is going down and then you start to pray more. If it had not been for the Lord.

When you have tried everything, and nothing seems to work, what a friend I have in Jesus. Will you try Him, come on you ought to try Him. As I look back over my life, everything happening back to back, but I made it. Would have never made it without You (God). I made it through, If it had not been for the Lord where would I be.

Sometimes you have problems in your life, and you come to a cliff, and you are scared to go on. But you can hear God saying Faye come to the cliff, but you still scared you going to fall over. But God says it again, come to the cliff and you go, and He pushes you over, and during the fall you realize you can fly. Look at God. All it takes is a little faith.

Matthew 17:20, "And Jesus said unto them, Because of your unbelief: for verily I say unto you, If ye have faith as a grain of mustard seed, ye shall say unto this mountain, Remove hence to yonder place; and it shall remove; and nothing shall be impossible unto you."

Acts 14-22, "Confirming the souls of the disciples and exhorting them to continue in the faith, and that we must through much tribulation enter into the kingdom of God."

I have seen storms and rain. But when leaning on Jesus, He has always come through. Nothing but the power of God can protect me.

John 1:7, "The same came for a witness, to bear witness of the Light, that all men through Him might believe

But we walk in the light as He is in the light, we have fellowship one with another, and the blood of Jesus cleanseth us from all our sin."

If it had not been for the Lord. So thankful that the God I serve trusts me to do His work. Thanks to my heavenly father. Yes, I will work for Him until He returns.

If you heard nothing, I have said know that God has your back, even if it's against the wall.

CHAPTER TWO

Get in Where You Fit In

I pray that you pray for me as I bring the word of God to you. Someone once told me not all preaching will be accepted, and not all preaching will be understood. However, you must continue to preach the word of God no matter how much opposition you face, you must stand boldly.

Get in where you fit in. As a church, we are here to preach the word of God, it may not come across as you want it but the Word is the Word. We can't sugar coat anything. There is always a place for you in the kingdom of God. I have felt loneliness but had everything I could want or need. But the loneliness without Christ, nothing can fill that, so I fitted in where I could, studying with different organizations, still lonely. But one day my best friend started with First Pentecostal Church. She invited me and I received the Holy Ghost. Life has not been the same since.

As growing in Christ, I fitted in where I could, not knowing during this time I was learning a lot. Then in 1995, I stepped out with the man of God that gave me Bible studies and started a church in a different city. What a time we had. The church is Landmark Pentecostal Church, and the man of God is Pastor Walter N. Willis, Jr., I fitted in where I could.

God showed us many blessings and miracles day in and day out. I can't express the gratitude and love we were introduced to.

There were times we did not think we would make it and times we thought we would lose our minds. But God. During this period God made us into what we are today. Fire baptized the power of the Holy Ghost. I would not trade this for anything in or out of this world. I fitted in where I could.

Jesus will never put anything on you that you cannot handle. I appreciate my heavenly father. Now I am grown in the Lord, not on milk anymore. I want to pass the torch on and let someone get in where they fit. Jesus is the right place to be. God created us to be a reflection of Him. Also, keep the vision of your pastor. Others may not see or feel it. But if you keep that same vision and step out on faith, God will show up and show out. I am encouraging you to step out in faith believing God has already supplied, healed, delivered, or showed your destiny. Walk in the Holy Ghost. Get in where you fit in. He is waiting for you.

CHAPTER THREE

Being Realistic

B eing Realistic is someone who has a good grip on the reality of a situation and understands what can and cannot be done, something that is a practical achievable ideal, or something that resembles the actual truth about life.

So, Is Jesus Real?

Trusting Him and knowing when He speaks to you is that realistic or is that just trusting in something that is not true.

There will be people when you tell them that God told you to move or do something and they are going to say to you I know God can do it, but you have to be realistic. Does being realistic mean, I stop doing what God said because someone says you must be realistic, or I continue to trust God and see what He is going to do. I chose to follow God's plan and step out by faith. Let me tell you when you are in the will of God, even if you have to walk alone, everything will fall in place and happen the way it is supposed to even if he has to use the people around you.

The pain of having to step out alone and trust God will make you closer to him. You have this battle of wanting to quit or throw your hands up, but then you remember the battle is not yours it is the Lord's. What an awesome God we serve.

I thank you for the battle that you are fighting for me. I could not make it without you. You are my strength, my refuge, and my secret

7

place. I can say I am in this battle, but I am not defeated. It seems like it, but I know God has me, completely.

Victory is won, rejoice for He is good and then there is a rest, "Selah". I do not know how long but during my Selah moment I am going to praise Him and thank Him for another chance to call Him by His name, Jesus. What an awesome God we serve, resting in Jesus is all I need.

So again, I say being realistic is trusting when God tells you to do something that you do it, even if you must do it yourself because He is real.

God will not ask anything of you and not supply every need, but you must put the action behind it. He speaks, you move.

During this battle, there may be many whisperings and just waiting for you to fail. But while all that is happening just proclaim God's word. Even when you try to hold back you want to be able to because it is the God you serve fighting a battle already won and it's God's word.

God takes our prayers and complaints that we bring to Him and He often answers our prayers just to correct our faulty thinking, so that we see things in the right way and so we can see we have no reason to worry in the first place. Psalm 23, Yes, I will trust him and love him and if He says go, I will go. Even if I feel defeated and put against a wall. If anyone will not God I will. Thank you, Lord, for trusting me to do your perfect will. I need you every day, guide my footsteps, and guard my tongue. To be like Jesus is all I want, Selah.

CHAPTER FOUR

Facing What the Enemy
Think Is Defeat

Y ou know sometimes everything around you seems to be crumbling up or tumbling down. Cannot find peace or you think your world is upside down.

But I can tell you when facing what the enemy thinks is defeat, God is in front of every situation, never behind anything. Look at Pharaoh's army wiped out. His people on the other side army behind them, God in front of them.

Job lost everything but not defeated. David hunted down but not defeated and looked at Jesus, crucified but not defeated. Why because He is God. My, my, my!

We must know that faith will bring you through if you trust God. Live and cherish what God has for you.

Sometimes we sit back and say what is wrong with this world, then you must realize the adversary is in this world and things are going to happen. Satan comes to steal, kill, and destroy so separate yourself from this world and things of this world that you know will interfere with your walk with God.

You look around people killing themselves or others, some because of the color of their skin. So much hatred, not enough love. These are signs of defeat by themselves, but I refuse to let the enemy have any part of me, not even my mind. Yes, Lord help me to love and trust you no matter what comes my way.

As we look at the news and see so much hatred, my heart bleeds, so heavy knowing someone has lost their child because of hatred and evil doing. At these times we must pray for forgiveness because if you are not careful it will put things in your heart that should not be there.

"God is love; and he that dwelleth in love dwelleth in God, and God in him." 1 John 4.

Love your neighbor no matter what they look like, treat them with respect.

One thing we are seeing these days is not love, but it takes one person to set a fire and one person to put out a flame.

Let us be the person who will set a fire in the name of Jesus. The world needs us to love like we never have before. It will be hard but great battles have been won during hard times. Let us trust God during this, teach our children to love despite and be an example for them. We as a people have to show love so that we can get love in return. Let us pray for our world and the people in it, and in authority. Cover them with prayer. Love when it is hard and show kind acts all the time. Let us make a difference in this world because our dad's name is Jesus. And Jesus will never turn his back on us no matter how we look or the color of our skin. He is a faithful God.

So, let's face what the enemy thinks is defeat, that is the love of a faithful God. You can love anybody, anywhere, no matter race, status, or anything else.

I want to be like Jesus. Teach me Oh Lord to be like you.

Love is the greatest gift of all.

CHAPTER FIVE

Prayer Must Be Sincere and Complete During These Perilous Time

We must find the time to pray when we are going through these perilous times the Bible speaks of such: 2 Timothy 3:1-5. "This know also, that in the last days perilous times shall come. For men shall be lovers of their own selves, covetous, boasters, proud, blasphemers, disobedient to parents, unthankful, unholy, Without natural affection, trucebreakers, false accusers, incontinent, fierce, despisers of those that are good, Traitors, heady, highminded, lovers of pleasures more than lovers of God; Having a form of godliness, but denying the power thereof: from such turn away."

I think about the steps to pray. These five steps have helped me get in touch with God, especially after a hard day of work.

The first step is Praise, it helps you overcome problems and clear your mind. The second step is praying, repent of all your sins, known and unknown. Ask God to forgive you every time you pray. The third step is cleaning my heart. I don't want a jealous spirit, help me not to be adultery or anything that is not like God. I want a pure heart and pure spirit not laziness, jealousy, anger, lust, or a selfish attitude. The fourth step is asking God to touch my mind, clean my mind, keep me to have peace of mind. Let that be in the past that is under the blood. Because God does not remember, help me to see things in the spirit. Let me memorize your word and move on in this world. Move on my brothers and sisters and all my loved ones. 5th, End your prayer with praise again thanking the almighty

God for everything and supplying your needs.

Listen the only way to overcome the power of Hell is prayer.

Luke 11:1-13, Philippians 2:6,7, Psalm 55:16,17. You must believe when you are praying, choose to pray which will bring glory to God. Prayer is the key to everything. Talk to God with supplication (God help me to pray, God give me the Holy Ghost) without communicating with God you find yourself lonely. You can be in a big family, married, have children, everyone around you, and still feel lonely.

It is natural to desire a conversation with God. Luke 11-1. The wiser a man, the greater is his prayer. Prayer is longing for God. Prayer changes things but most importantly prayer needs to change the individuals that are praying. The greatest thing you can do for your church is to pray. Praying is not a beggar; it is a binder. Be serious when you pray. The greatest success in prayer is to do it and let God have His way in your life,

You can defeat Satan with what you have. 11Corinthians 10:1-4.

Putting on the whole armor of God Ephesians 6. We must put on the armor to fight against the devil. Get some guts until you win the battle. No matter what you say I am going to win this battle, do not run from the battle, stand, and fight with prayer.

Prayer is a spiritual exercise, the more you use it the stronger you are. You are in this world but not of the world. The world is not our friend. The world is God's enemy. God hates sin but loves sinners. If we rub shoulders with the world, we become an enemy with God. The flesh is the nature we receive within us when we were born to this world. The flesh is the biggest problem. We contain the carnal sinful nature of our parents. We receive this sinful nature from the Garden of Eden. When the fruit was eaten (devil) the flesh became carnal. Galatians 5-17. Flesh tells you to backslide. It will destroy you and you will not be able to get back to the place you once were. Keep yourself pure, Malachi 3:7

God has given us the weapon to overcome temptation. James 1:14. Every man is tempted, that is why prayer is the answer. A family that prays together, stays together. The Word of God will save you. Let us pray for each other and know God will do what He says He will do. Trust my God!

CHAPTER SIX

The Doors Are Open, Where Is the Church

N o one comes into a building without coming through a door. It is either open for you or you opened it. But to gain access to any building you have to make your way through the door. Coming through those doors is the second part of becoming the Church, of course having the Holy Ghost is the first part.

I used the door because we do not want our relationship with God to be an open door. Now do not get me wrong, God has set before us an open door amid all these tough times, but the open door I am referring to right now is the eye to your soul and spirit. Be the Church.

Who or what doors have tried to shut doors against your life? Who has said it's over for you? Act 12:11-14 says that Peter had been put in prison. King Herod had been pursuing his life for destruction (see this open door brings destruction) but an angel came and delivered Peter out of the prison (an angel delivered Peter from that open door, God sent the Church to help Peter). In this season you must be persistent, you must push. You must press forth until something happens. You are close to your breakthrough. Do not be the door, be the Church. Your enemies shall be excited concerning what God is about to do in your life. Herod never believed that Peter would break out of that prison, likewise, your enemies may think you are still jobless, still homeless, still sick, still in poverty, still depressed, but they shall be surprised, you are not in the same place they thought they left you, you closed that door of doubt and became the Church. Luke 15:1-10.

I would like to say it was the sorrow of my childhood, and how sorry I was for all the pain, shame, and financial hardship we had. I would like to say I had come to see the error of my ways, that I realized what a fool I had been not realizing that I was an open door.

I would love to tell you I have gotten everything right but sorry to tell you I have a long way to go, so I confess my wrongdoing and love God like never before.

You are probably wondering why I am telling you this, and maybe you are wondering what difference it makes. Well, this world is divided by so much greed and suffering in a country where many doors are closed, where the governments throw rocks and hide their hands.

But I am here to tell you when one door closes, two doors open. You cannot have doubt and faith at the same time. There is no way. You are either going to trust God at his word or you are not. Psalm 121!

I will lift my eyes to the hills from whence comes my help, my help comes from the Lord, who made heaven and earth.

The doors are open, where is the Church. We are in our last days, just going with the motion. I want to be the Church. When others see me, they should say I want what she has, or they should say you inspire me to do right or change my ways. The Church loves when it gets hard. The Church will turn the other cheek. The Church is in us.

During these perilous times do not get caught up being an open door but be the church. My soul waits for the Lord.

Let us focus on pleasing God during this time, because I see miracle after miracle, blessings on blessings, and to be part of this you must be the church. I want to be the church and I will work for Him until Hi return.

When you see God moving in your life, hold on to that. Trust Him keep walking, fall, get up, and try it again. There is nothing too hard fo God. You heard of this old saying when life throws you lemons, mak lemonade. Right now, it's time to love your enemies, walk in the Hol Ghost, give a helping hand and do whatever you can for the Lord. Whe you feel like giving up, push that much harder. You know I look at Job now he was the church, no matter what, he kept his integrity to God.

I need everyone to focus on the vision now. Our vision is to help hurting world and offer ourselves as a living sacrifice.

God is taking you this year to another level. We are getting there The world can never measure the standard of a child of God. The expectation of your enemies shall be brought to nothing. We are the Church. Get ready for opened doors for victory. A door is a place o transition. The first door is being the church.

This is the time between you and God. So, let us choose God and the vision that is put upon us. I humbly say I want to be the Church.

Thank you and God bless you all!

CHAPTER SEVEN

It Is Morning; Time to Get Up

As I write this message, I can see myself underwater, but when you are underwater you learn to dog paddle to keep yourself afloat.

Strong winds may be blowing against us, but you have to push against the wind even if you have to turn backward. Keep pushing, stepping over things that will try to hold you back, step right over it, go around jump and keep going.

It is morning; time to get up. 1King 19:4-8

Now Ellijah had just been through one of the greatest tests of God at this point. He just came through the shutdown with the prophets of Baal and God showed up victoriously. How many know when God shows up, He always wins. He then went down to the river and killed them all, but just as soon as he heard that Jezebel was after him, he ran off. This is where we find him – now, under the juniper tree. And the angel said to him "Arise and eat."

Joshua 7:9-11

"For the Canaanites and all the inhabitants of the land shall hear of it, and shall environ us round, and cut off our name from the earth: and what wilt thou do unto thy great name? And the Lord said unto Joshua, Get thee up; wherefore liest thou thus upon thy face? Israel hath sinned, and they have also transgressed my covenant which I commanded them:

for they have even taken of the accursed thing, and have also stolen, and dissembled also, and they have put it even among their own stuff."

It is time to get up!

There is a time to laugh and a time to cry. But right now, it's time to get up. Many are the afflictions of the righteous, but the Lord shall deliver them out of them all. If you dwell in the past, then you will die in the past.

Many of us are allowing something that happened to us 5 years ago; even yesterday drag us down and beat us up. Just as the Lord said to Elijah, and Joshua get thee up. Get up!

Paul said this one thing I do, forgetting those things which are behind, I press toward the mark for the prize of the most high calling of God in Christ Jesus.

It is a lie from the pits of hell, to keep you bound up and angry about something that happened years ago or ongoing that you put yourself in. Forget all the battles that you have lost.

We have got to learn to deal with the issues from our past, to move forward into what God would have us to become.

It is morning, time to get up!

"In this world, you will have tribulations, but be of good cheer, for I have overcome the world," I have decided to trust the Lord no matter what. I am going through and in return. I can hear Him say Faye arise and shine for your light has come and the glory of the Lord has risen upon you.

Do not call to mind former things or ponder things of the past. Behold I will do something new, now it will spring forth; will you not be aware of it?

He said He will make a roadway in the wilderness, rivers, and deserts. To give drink to His chosen people. I want to be among the chosen.

You can look into some people's faces, and it looks like you lost your joy. Do not feel the sense of excitement and wonder you felt in your early Christian years, but you know the good thing about that is God understands, and He has provided some ways for you to get your joy back. You just can't sit in a fired-up service, you have to praise and worship him.

Singing and shouting to the Lord can turn the heaviness of the heart into joy. I know I wanted to throw my hands up and say I give up, **But God** always makes a way. When you start to rejoice in the Lord it becomes contagious. Try it, and you will catch it.

Let see if you remember the story of Jonah. I know he was ready for his morning. See Jonah, of course, was on a boat. The weather was speaking a message, you know God speaks to us all through different and unique things or weather patterns that some say made history.

It is time to get up. Ok, listen I want you to hear this. The men on the boat said it is a very unusual storm. We have never seen anything like this, that is all I hear on the news. There must be a reason for this; they connected the dots and discovered Jonah and his God was the reason for the storm. Hmmmmm

The Storm only stopped when they threw Jonah overboard, Jonah being thrown overboard represents the dying of himself will because Jonah had no idea a fish would eat him. He expected death. In the belly of the fish, Jonah cried out in the hottest prayer meeting he ever had. No one around just him and God. I can hear him say; I am here God; I give myself to you. He is now praying with sincerity, passion, and conviction. It is time to get up.

God knew Jonah was praying. God knew I was praying to save my life. When you have been in the belly of the fish you come out a different person, you will serve and obey God with joy. Coming out is a great morning. You won't care who is sitting beside you, mama, daddy, husband, wife, or children, you are going to praise Him. It is morning, it's time to get up. Whatever the Lord wants from me, I will do wholeheartedly. Like Jonah people are watching what you say yes to and what you say no to. People are healed by the power of God when you say yes and get thrown overboard into the will of God.

CHAPTER EIGHT

Benefits of Pain and Suffering

S uffering prepares you for the increase. It helps us to learn important life lessons. Deuteronomy 32: 10, 11 He found him in a desert land, and in the waste howling wilderness; he led him about, he instructed him, he kept him as the apple of his eye. As an eagle stirreth up her nest, fluttereth over her young, spreadeth abroad her wings, taketh them, beareth them on her wings:) Mother eagle forcing her baby out of the nest to teach it to fly.

Pain and suffering can bring about creativity, resourcefulness, and courage (parents who lost a child, or loved one, or maybe your loved one hanging on for life, a sister or brother dying spiritually). 2 Corinthians 1:3-5, "Blessed be God, even the Father of our Lord Jesus Christ, the Father of mercies, and the God of all comfort; Who comforteth us in all our tribulation, that we may be able to comfort them which are in any trouble, by the comfort wherewith we ourselves are comforted of God. For as the sufferings of Christ abound in us, so our consolation also aboundeth by Christ."

Pain and suffering can help shape our character. People who have survived through tough times not knowing if they are going to make it, have a strength of character which is admired by others. God is refined by the fire which heats it until the impurities come out. Isaiah 48:10,

"Behold, I have refined thee, but not with silver; I have chosen thee in the furnace of affliction", Zechariah 13:8-9, "And it shall come to pass, that in all the land, saith the Lord, two parts therein shall be cut off and die; but the third shall be left therein. And I will bring the third part through the fire, and will refine them as gold is tried: they shall call on my name, and I will hear them: I will say, It is my people: and they shall say, The LORD is my God", James 1: 2-4, "My brethren, count it all joy when ye fall into divers temptations; Knowing this, that the trying of your faith worketh patience. But let patience have her perfect work, that ye may be perfect and entire, wanting nothing."

During this pain trust God and know He is God.

Pain and suffering can test us to show what we are made of. Abraham, Job, and Peter were tested. The testing showed the weakness and strengths of their faith in God. Genesis 22: 1-4 describes Abraham's test. The entire book of Job was a test for him. Matthew 26:69-75, tells where Peter failed, and he learned something about himself. Peter learned you can be close to Jesus, even walking with him and there can be a little something in you, that you must go through pain or suffering to bring it out. He denied Christ, I think Peter was afraid and cared more about what others would say or do. But when he saw the one, he loved going through pain and suffering he could not take it anymore. It leads you to repentance for your salvation

Sometimes it takes pain and suffering to turn a person's life around and head it in the right direction.

Pain and suffering can sometimes help us to trust God more. We are forced to turn to God because we have no other place to turn. Job 40:3-5, "Then Job answered the LORD, and said, Behold, I am vile; what shall I answer thee? I will lay mine hand upon my mouth. Once have I spoken; but I will not answer: yea, twice; but I will proceed no further.", Lamentations 3:19-24, Habakkuk 3:17-19.

Bearing pain and suffering can be an inspiration to others. We must be able to take our thorns in the flesh, so we will be able to take the message of Christ to many people around us.

Pain and suffering can divine purpose in preparing us for glory, which will make you humble and ready for external glory. Lord help me to do thy will. 2 Corinthian 4: 6-18

Pain and suffering can prevent us from becoming proud in spirit. When you hurt the thorn in the flesh will remind you to humble yourself, you are nothing.

I will decrease so my God will increase, 2 Corinthian 12:7-10.

Most of all Pain and suffering can allow us to be like Jesus. Love in spite of. When people come against you love anyway. Thank you, Lord, for my pain and suffering. Philippians 3:8-11, Hebrews 2:9-11, 4:15: 1 Peter 4: 12-16.

Promises of help for God's People in times of suffering. Deuteronomy 32:10,11, Psalm 9:9-10, Psalm 46:1-3, Isaiah 41:10, Lamentations 3:19-26,33, John 16:33, Romans 6:5

CHAPTER NINE

Through Your Pain and Sufferin

When you have a chance to look back, thank God for what He has allowed to happen, rather it's good or bad. Give Him thanks. How many can say, I trust you Lord and really mean it? Seems like everything around you tumbling down, not knowing which way to turn and you realize you must submit to God. Pain and suffering, thank God for it. Without it, we would not need God, because we would think we were perfect and already saved.

Yes, I tried talking to someone about lots of things that happen in my life, all they would do is come back negative, or you cannot do this or because you did this. I let the person talk and I said God I don't accept that, this is for my good, give me the strength to endure. Lord over the years I have built monuments rather it was prayers, tears, or giving. Can you use what I have stored up this time Lord? And yes, Lord I know you owe me nothing. But my faith will see this through. This saying has always been in my spirit, "when you are down to nothing, God is up to something." You never know what God's plan is until it happens sometimes, I like to say He had a ram in the bush.

Through my pain and suffering, I can now say I trust Him and can depend on Him. Yes, I had people all around but still felt alone because I have trust problems, but when God steps in, you know it.

And I am not talking about just suffering because of a child, being tripped down to nothing, bank account garnished, not a penny left, bills bouncing after writing checks because the money was not there. My husband was mad at creditors for taking his hard-earned money.

I trusted God, some people offered to give us money until everything would be worked out. I said "NO" God will work it out. If God got His part (tithes), I do not care about the rest. Let me tell you what God did the very next week. Someone gave us the total amount to put in our account, six months later checks had been garnished (both) my husband let me go to school at night and did not say all bills were behind. But back to the story, I'm at work when my boss calls me to the front office and says, "As long as I have been doing this, I have never seen a creditor write someone a check for what they were garnished." Of course, I said that is my God. I received about 4 or 5 checks for $600.00 or more. The administrator and D.O.N. was amazed. Do not tell me what God can't do during your pain and suffering.

Since then God has put me in his favor, and I wear it in humility, not a proud spirit. It seems like every time I turn around; He is blessing me. But I made a promise, when I get blessed, I will bless someone else and I have kept my word. And no, I do not go around parading, what I do, because that is not of God. I give it and walk away. And it helps me to do it this way because I am human, and I want to do it in the spirit and allow God to use me where He sees fit. Plus, I can say I am doing it for God and not man.

If you hear nothing I am saying, hear this you must surrender all, submit and trust God through every situation, rather you understand or not. Wait I say wait on the Lord, He will come through.

As I close this testimony, I want to know what is the thorn in your flesh or spirit?

CHAPTER TEN

Success in the People's Business

Philippians 4:13

Success is a difficult word to define. Each person must determine for himself/herself what amount to fulfillment in their life. God will succeed for us, not defeat us. Success has to do with what is inside a person, it's an inside job.

It is relative to our thoughts and attitudes, for they make us what we are. Positive thoughts toward success, while negative thoughts will guide one toward failure. Which is the dominant thought pattern in your life, positive or negative?

Some jobs related us straight to people, they are our stock and trade, must have them to work. We are people dealers. Our success will be determined by how well we can get along with other people and influence them for the cause of Christ.

There are no church failures, only people failures. Every man has his likes and dislikes. Some people you must handle with kid gloves, others with a long handle spoon or manhandled. A wise leader will be able to learn the difference.

Proverb 24:5, "A wise man is strong; yea, a man of knowledge increaseth strength."

Knowledge is what a leader must keep when helping people. Do not be too forceful, but graceful.

Engage with each person differently. No two people are the same. Some may come to you and hurt your feelings. What are you going to do cry, fuss back, or frown? Let me tell you what happened to me while working for my God. I got spit in the face, with sniff spit. I wiped it off and kept telling this woman about God. She did not mean to she was talking with it in her mouth. (inside I was about to throw-up). But she could not tell how I was feeling. Be forbearing even when people seem at their worst. And you know being a leader is dedicating yourself to God in season or out of season. Being faithful honoring the Man of God. Willing to say I will do it even if no one else will.

My Pastor has always told us it's going to be people that are going to make you mad, upset, and almost make you want to curse. But stand back THINK before you open your mouth. Words can cut like a sword and wound that person for life. They can dish it out but cannot take it, l like some would say. So, pray and ask God to help your mental attitude and behavior also. And prepare your mind for action.

1 Peter 1:13," Wherefore gird up the loins of your mind, be sober, and hope to the end for the grace that is to be brought unto you at the revelation of Jesus Christ:"

Some people you talk to are so grouchy. You speak to them; they turn around with a frown on their face like you have done something to them. But you know if we do not watch it some of us leaders can be like that. Keep a smile on your face even if you think you are going through the worst trial ever. What business are we in?

I am going to tell you I am going to praise God. Leaders let the Holy Ghost prick your spirit. Keep a service going. Leaders pray before they leave home so when they walk in church or somewhere, they are ready to fight anything they need to spiritually. Leaders pray for others in the church when altar call, leaders do not have to be told to come to pray, they know their position. Leaders will keep the order; they are eyes for the Pastor.

Leaders must learn to place their desires on the altar. A good leader knows where to go in times of trouble (altar). A leader must bear their own cross. Place it all on the altar and let nothing come between them and the Lord. A leader will do what needs to be done even if you do not feel like doing it. They will say yes sir, yes ma'am sure I can. Stay motivated and determined.

I like this part. I have a shovel around here if you want to dig yourself up.

Men lead your home also, women just because you are a leader in your church or organization does not mean you are a leader in your home. Be submissive to your husband. Being a leader if your husband decides he does not approve of what you are doing in a public place keep a smile on your face, plus keep in mind, he leads the family. Later in private, let him know you did not agree. If you are blessed to have a husband in a leadership position with you being greatly used by God together, count your blessings.

Be used by the Lord.

CHAPTER ELEVEN

What God Means to Me

1Peter 1:8-9

Psalms 118:24, "This is the day which the Lord hath made; we will rejoice and be glad in it."

Isaiah 61:10, "I will greatly rejoice in the LORD, my soul shall be joyful in my God; for He hath clothed me with the garments of salvation, He hath covered me with the robe of righteousness, as a bridegroom decketh himself with ornaments, and as a bride adorneth herself with her jewels."

Philippians 4:4, "Rejoice in the Lord always: and again, I say, Rejoice."

1 Thessalonians 5: 16-18, "Rejoice evermore. Pray without ceasing. In everything give thanks: for this is the will of God in Christ Jesus concerning you."

Joy is the first thing that comes to mind when I think about Jesus. Growing into a mature Christian who follows the Holy Ghost is not something that happens overnight, it is a learning process that takes time and patience. Little by little, one experience after another God tries and tests our emotions, giving us opportunities to grow.

Every trial or situation I went through or going through I threw up my hands and said Lord I surrender; I give it to you and leave it with him. Yes, I might be sad, hurt, or whatever but my Joy I keep. God allows us to go through difficult times or situations that stir up our emotions. In this way, we can see for ourselves how emotionally unstable we can be and how desperately we need the help of the Lord. With His help, we can make it through our emotional trials. The mind is a terrible thing to waste. Always let us have the mind of Christ Jesus, whether you are happy or sad. Jesus came so we might have life. Let us live and not die. Trust the Lord and He will take away for you. He did it for me. Thought my mind was going to go, because of so much hurt and disappointment. Thinking people on your side and you hear the words that prick your soul. But then you remember Jesus was not led by His feelings when He died on the cross. How can I let my feelings interrupt my relationship with God and others?

Once you feel the peace of God, Joy stays in your spirit, no matter what you are going through. I don't know about you, but I need my heavenly Father at all times. So yes, joy is the first thing for me and there are so many other ways: love, happiness.

It feels like Christmas when I think about my Lord. Opening a new gift every time I call His name. It is like I cannot get enough. So hungry for Jesus my plate is not full, I want more of Him. Every time I mention His name.

Let us trust Him at all times and count it all joy. Here is a song we used to sing when I was a baby in Christ.

J-E-S-U-S
HE IS MY LORD AND KING
J-E-S-U-S
HE IS MY EVERYTHING

J-E-S-U-S
WHAT THAT NAME
JESUS

YES LORD, YOU ARE EVERYTHING TO ME FOREVER

CHAPTER TWELVE

Giving Grace With the Words You Speak
Hebrew 3:13

God wants us to encourage each other because He knows we need it. We live in this world that has put some of us toward selfishness and despair. Sin steals joy, bodies break down, our plans go through, our dreams die, our resolve weakens, our perspective dims no light anywhere. But the Bible says we are promised to suffer, 1 Peter 4:12," Beloved, think it not strange concerning the fiery trial which is to try you, as though some strange thing happened unto you:"

Persecution John 15:20," Remember the word that I said unto you, the servant is not greater than his Lord. If they have persecuted me, they will also persecute you; if they have kept my saying, they will keep yours also."

2 Timothy 3:12," Yea, and all that will live godly in Christ Jesus shall suffer persecution and trials." James 1:2-3," My brethren, count it all joy when ye fall into divers temptations; Knowing this, that the trying of your faith worketh patience."

Encouragement is not the material things you have accomplished but it is the hope that it will lift someone's heart toward the Lord

Colossians 4:8 Whom I have sent unto you for the same purpose, that he might know your estate, and comfort your hearts;)

It shows grace and that everything is in His control. Encouragement is an important way of giving grace to each other.

Pray and ask God to let you help someone. Ask Him to give you the heart to love your enemies and pray for everyone. Be the person someone wants to be around, someone that will make the church flourish and see things happen.

Encouragement should come naturally if you are a child of God, and especially with the Holy Ghost because God is love. Love everyone and try to encourage anyone you encounter. Be humble and expect nothing in return. Ask God to help you fan the flame, wherever you are. But one thing to remember, if someone does not accept your encouragement do not get discouraged. Just keep doing it, sometimes it does not happen overnight. It takes longer on some people, but I promise they feel your encouraging spirit. God is love and love never to give up on anyone. So, let us not give up on our neighbor.

I encourage you to pray for this special gift. Because love is about all. Love is the greatest of all. Stay close to God. Make a difference in someone's life today. PUSH until something happens. Do not stop because God will not stop us.

CHAPTER THIRTEEN

During Covid-19 Panic
Psalms 33:11-22

E verything closing, infection rates increasing, death rising every day schools closing, workplace, and even some churches.

Sometimes news like this can make you a little worried o fearful. Worrying is an act of fear and evidence of a lack of faith. God knows sometimes we will have these feelings. That is why He said it i His Word so many times. DO NOT FEAR repeatedly. DO NOT FEAR and DO NOT BE AFRAID. He does not condemn us for our fear. He encourages us in His Word over and over to be of good courage. He wil never leave or forsake us. As you face fear or worry during this coronavirus just trust God and know He commands us to "be bold, be strong" because He is with us.

Every day I encourage you to get up and pray, read the word o God, and praise Him. This will help and retrain your brain to trust ir God and not walk in fear. God is looking at us every day, He has no forgotten about His people.

But at this time, I honestly think God is trying to get our attention that sin cannot be the first in our lives. God wants to be the first thing i ur lives. So much sin in this world right now. And just like the days of Noah, no one is seeing this.

People it is going to rain (pandemic) and the doors are going to lose. Get on board and know God will do just what He said He would do. Now is the time to choose Jesus. Realize no king is saved by the size of his army. We wait in hope for the Lord, He is our help and our shield. Trust in the Lord always. Yes, during this COVID-19. Make sure you trust God with all your heart and that He will see us through, no matter which way this thing goes. Remember being and living for the Lord does not exempt us from going through this, but at least we can trust Him to go with us through it.

Thank you, Lord, for not doing this without us. Thank you for letting this change our lives and encourage us to live for you and trust you even more.

John 14:26, "But the Comforter, which is the Holy Ghost, whom the Father will send in my name, he shall teach you all things, and bring all things to your remembrance, whatsoever I have said unto you."

Just know the Holy Ghost (our helper) is with us. God will come and save us according to Isaiah 35:4, "Say to them that are of a fearful heart, Be strong, fear not: behold, your God will come with vengeance, even God with a recompense; he will come and save you).

Another scripture comes to mind." Psalms 23:4, "Yea, though I walk through the valley of the shadow of death, I will fear no evil: for thou art with me; thy rod and thy staff they comfort me."

You know in this valley; God is with us. Not sure what is going to happen next, but one thing I do know He will not leave us. This is a pruning time. Everything that is happening is biblical, know that God is real, and His Word is His Word, and He will return soon.

The doors are opened now! Do not wait! Run in!

Accept the Lord right now and receive His precious Gift (Holy Ghost).

Acts 2:38," Then Peter said unto them, Repent, and be baptized every one of you in the name of Jesus Christ for the remission of sins and ye shall receive the gift of the Holy Ghost."

Take heed and hear the word of the Lord.

CHAPTER FOURTEEN

What Does It Mean to Trust God

Proverb 3:5

Everybody always says trust God. And all at the same time, that is what you think you are doing. So, tell me what is trust?

The dictionary says a firm belief in the reliability, truth, ability, or strength of someone or something.

But trusting God does not mean that. Because you can believe everything going your way and it does not.

Some people are killed for believing and trusting God. And then people start not having enough faith or think God is not holding up on His end. But you must know God reigns on the just and unjust. God is a miracle worker, but He will let you go through things. The Disciples were walking with Jesus and still were tortured and murdered for believing in the truth. One was sent to an isolated island in his old age. Just letting you know suffering and pain is something everyone must face, whether you believe or trust in God.

You know God does not owe us any explanation when life is painful or not going our way. So, trust in God no matter what happens. Turn to Him instead of away from Him. Even despite these things, trusting in God is the right way to go. Keep praying, even when those prayers seem to have no effect. You keep saying like Job "The Lord gives, and the Lord takes away. Blessed be the name of the Lord.

So, trusting God is the right way, because if we can accept things are from the hand of God. It will help you live with less stress and provide you with hope. I know it is easier said than done. But continue to do so. Things are going to come, let it come but in the midst know God will do what He said he would do. He is always with us.

I have learned I rather have Him by my side, than not to have Him at all. Trust means that even when I am hurt or in pain, God is right there. I trust God will see me through. So, believe God has a plan during this dark time in our world.

Lean toward Jesus everyone, because that is the way to go.

CHAPTER FIFTEEN

Gossip and Backbitting

Matthew 22;39, John 17:11

When you accept Jesus, receive the Holy Ghost we become new creatures in Christ, we also become the Bride of Christ. So, at this time we become brothers and sisters because we have the same Father, we become family. We all are different in personality, talents, and abilities. Everyone has a part.

You must stand strong because some have sheep clothing and spirit like wolves. These will tell you about another sister or brother, what they are doing or not doing. Be careful because if they can tell you these things, **you are next in line!**

They will go tell the same person the same thing about you. It is better to ask to not talk about your family. I call this **HOLY GOSSIP**. They think because they use God's word, or say, "I am not talking about nobody but……." If they are not what just happened? Do not be a part of Holy Gossip.

Gossip is gossiping no matter where it comes from. This is the sin we commit, which drives people away from the church where people are supposed to come and let God heal them.

Guys backbiting is one of Satan's weapons because He always attacks from behind and when our back is turned. He is a coward because the Bible says to go to the person and make it right.

Backbiters are men that can pretend they love everyone but deep inside, always have something to say about somebody as soon as they walk away. That tongue is like fire and it makes that person corrupted and they think they are right because they want to use God's word and say I am not talking about her/him. Shame on you.

It only takes one person to be a back biter and it corrupts the whole church and its growth in the Lord.

But Jesus said "he who is not with me is against me, and he who does not gather with me scatters." Matt 12:30

Are we building up the body of Christ with words or tearing it down?

The tongue has the power of life and death, and those who love it will eat its fruit. Proverbs 18:21

So, learn to tame your tongue and find something good to say. A bad mouth comes from a bad heart. Change your heart and tame your tongue. Speak life to your brothers and sisters. Because you are family now. You will give account for this on judgment day, for every careless word you have spoken.

Change your heart today, whatever comes out of your mouth is in your heart, be like Jesus. No matter who you are or what position you are in, be careful and wise, stop straddling the fence. It is time to clean the house and think before you open your mouth.

There is always a way of having unity when you put ungodly things to the side. Love one another as Christ loves His church.

Let us be like Jesus. A family that prays together stays together. Be my family, I need a loving family to lean on when I am going through or just to have a small talk and sometimes a hug.

CHAPTER SIXTEEN

Being Used by God

I just want to know can God use me? Acts 9:1-6,10-16.
¹Threatenings and slaughter against the disciples of the Lord, went to unto the high priest,

² And desired of him letters to Damascus to the synagogues, that if he found any of this way, whether they were men or women, he might bring them bound unto Jerusalem.

³ And as he journeyed, he came near Damascus: and suddenly there shined round about him a light from heaven:

⁴ And he fell to the earth, and heard a voice saying unto him, Saul, Saul, why persecutest thou me?

⁵ And he said, Who art thou, Lord? And the Lord said, I am Jesus whom thou persecutest: it is hard for thee to kick against the pricks.

⁶ And he trembling and astonished said, Lord, what wilt thou have me to do? And the Lord said unto him, Arise, and go into the city, and it shall be told thee what thou must do.

¹⁰ And there was a certain disciple at Damascus, named Ananias; and to him said the Lord in a vision, Ananias. And he said, Behold, I am here, Lord.

[11] And the Lord said unto him, Arise, and go into the street which is called Straight, and enquire in the house of Judas for one called Saul, of Tarsus: for, behold, he prayeth,

[12] And hath seen in a vision a man named Ananias coming in, and putting his hand on him, that he might receive his sight.

[13] Then Ananias answered, Lord, I have heard by many of this man, how much evil he hath done to thy saints at Jerusalem:

[14] And here he hath authority from the chief priests to bind all that call on thy name.

[15] But the Lord said unto him, Go thy way: for he is a chosen vessel unto me, to bear my name before the Gentiles, and kings, and the children of Israel:

[16] For I will shew him how great things he must suffer for my name's sake.

Yes, I can be used by God, because it depends on the relationship that I have with Him, and my attitude.

Before Paul could be used, he had to get saved and willing to give his heart, life, and soul to God Just because a person is saved and knows the Lord, does not necessarily qualify him/her for service. The attitude must be right. So, sitting back I as myself are you mature, are you flexible, is your attitude, right? Are you willing to do what you do for Christ's sake, and not your glory?

Here is an example: when a saved person gets blessed and they parade around the church, money or material things in front of everyone. Instead of just saying God blessed our home and I want to give Him the glory. Do not boast to make someone else praise you and see what you have. If you do, that is your reward from man and not God.

Do not get me wrong it is good to testify what God has done for you. But be careful how and why you do what you do. Check yourself and make sure you are doing it for God, and you do not need approval from man. So, with that being said three things are important when it comes to being used by God: attitude, attitude, and attitude.

1 Corinthians 9:17, "For if I do this thing willingly I have a reward."

A wrong attitude: the brother that stayed at home in the Prodigal son and then complained because they celebrated the return of his sinful brother was like a lot of religious people. He did everything right but with the wrong spirit. He was like a beautiful apple that had rotten on the inside. He looked good on the outside, but he was rotten to the very heart,

There are some of God's people who are like that. They have all the right things on, looking good on the outside- they know all the right words and praises, but the attitude is all wrong. God helps us to have the right attitude.

My prayer is that the Lord teaches His people to examine themselves from inside out and love and do God's will with the right attitude.

So yes, we can all be used by God with the right attitude inside and outside. Teach me Oh Lord to be like you.

CHAPTER SEVENTEEN

Miracles Still Happens

Philippians 3: 1-11

This scripture let us know that Paul was a walking miracle. Look at Paul's life before (killing Christians) and God still performed miracles with and through him. His name had to change and be written in heaven. When God changes you, oh my change that will be (Paul name became Saul)

Circumcision is neither good nor bad unless it is something done to make one righteous before God. It is not wrong to make sacrifices or bear marks of devotion to God, because these things only become a problem when we make our salvation upon them. You can not put requirements on God, He is salvation. No other way, it must be God's way.

But back to Paul, If Paul can be part of a miracle you know someone like me or us, can know that miracles still happen.

Another miracle in the Bible, a woman was sick with uncontrolled bleeding, which made her spiritually unclean. She believes that Jesus is powerful enough to heal her. So that she would just need to touch his garments. But look at how she approaches Jesus; she comes from behind and touches his garments. She does not think herself worthy of even being addressed by Him.

But after she touches Jesus, He stops and asks who touched his garment. My, my, my exactly right there, it is a miracle.

He knew who touched Him and that He was healing her, of course, He is God. God has a habit of inviting people to come and enter a relationship with him rather than just ask you to come. He wanted to allow the woman to come face to face with her Savior. Because remember she came from behind not thinking she was worthy. But this tells us that Jesus can heal the unhealable. And He calls this woman His daughter despite her statue and aliment. He came to her as family. When we do not think we are worthy, Jesus says yes, we are, and miracles still happen.

Sometimes the struggle between faith and fear, Christ reminds us that we should not fear because our faith is what He brings to us even when we are overcome with fear, our God does not give up on us but continues to give us faith, reminding us of the promises that we place our faith in.

I am so glad Jesus is my peace and I am a miracle in Him. Thank you God I am a miracle of a changed life. I am not what I used to be. I trust you now and my faith is in you. God, I have no hesitation in my faith, I know who you are and what you can do.

Just looking back at my life, I know He is real. Can you say the same thing? What was the scariest time in your life? Did He bring you through? What comfort did faith bring you? And how has God used that situation in your faith life?

When you get the answer to these questions, ask yourself if miracles still happen.

CHAPTER EIGHTEEN

Prayer

Roman 8: 1-11, Ephesians 5:19-21

I know you will say you heard it before. Do not listen to that or do not listen to this. So, we are not going that route. Let us tell you what the Word of God says, and His Word does not come back void.

You have three enemies in the world that will try to get you in any way it can. (1) The world, peer pressure to like some else. (2) The Devil tries to sneak into your minds which you know the mind is a battlefield. You will say I am not going to do this or do that and you slip up and your hands and feet start going to places and doing things that you should not be doing.

Satan whispering, "It won't hurt, it is okay to do a little of this and that." (3) Self is the last thing you, yourself just decided what I want to do. Let us keep it real. I want to ask you this question, what if Jesus would have said let me keep it real? I do not want to be unpleasing to my God. He died on the cross so we could be saved. Where would we be today if He gave up on us and refused to go on the cross? Because He is all-powerful and He could have changed the whole situation if He wanted to. But because He loved us, He died for us. We must have a made-up mind. So no to the world, no the Devil, and no to the flesh or self.

Let us promise to look toward God and mind the things of God. Clean our hearts and minds and know that we serve a loving and kind God.

Prayer needs to be an everyday tool that we use, morning, noon, and night and in between if you need it. Prayer is the answer. Pray without ceasing. Love God with All your heart and focus on Jesus.

CHAPTER NINETEEN

Answered Prayers

Maybe you have been asking God to meet a pressing need or grant a particular desire, yet nothing seems to be happening. When this happens most Christians (saved folks) are tempted to give up.

If you want your prayer answered stop complaining and pointing fingers when something is not going as it should. Come on you know sometimes we have it bad. I know I do.

Isaiah 58:9," Then shalt thou call, and the Lord shall answer; thou shalt cry, and he shall say, here I am. If thou take away from the midst of thee the yoke, the putting forth of the finger and speaking vanity."

Matthew 7:2, "For with what judgment ye judge, ye shall be judged; and with what measure ye mete, it shall be measured to you again."

Matthew 7:6-8, "Give not that which is holy unto the dogs, neither cast ye your pearls before swine, lest they trample them under their feet, and turn again and rend you.

Ask, and it shall be given you; seek, and ye shall find; knock, and it shall be opened unto you; For every one that asketh receiveth; He that seeketh findeth; and to Him that knocketh it shall be opened."

Do not throw Holy things in front of the devil, the power of words will stop prayers from being answered.

I was talking to someone and I said we ask God for healing, financial and other things but no results, your words will hinder prayers. It is because you have to say, "Okay God what is wrong here?" I know I have been praying. Will you forgive me and show me what I am doing? Examine me O Lord, and then He will open doors that have been closed. Our homes or churches will blossom, people will knock each other over trying to get through the doors because the anointing will draw them. Be careful of the words we speak that impact others around us.

Proverbs 12:18 there is that speaketh like the piercings of a sword: But the tongue of the wise is health.

Deuteronomy 1:11, "The Lord God of your fathers make you a thousand times so many more are you, and bless you, as hath promised you!"

As I was writing is a story; what came to me was walking the mile and being a committed leader. Successful leaders are not always highly gifted or intelligent people. A leader is anyone who uses their talent or position to get the job done, and the ability to work with others.

From the beginning to the present most of us have walked the mile. My, My, My! As I looked back God said there would be a change, and some of us do not see the change, stop looking with our natural eyes and look with our spiritual eyes. I do not know about you but while walking this mile and being a committed leader, I can see the blessing in everything, the ones already answered and the ones that are going to be answered. We have had prayers answered. It is revival time.
You know let me just take a minute and remind us about some of our answered prayers.

1. When you thought you were not going to make it, you had to let something go.

2. Sometimes you must lose something to gain and focus on your miracle.

3. You must through the hurt and the pain, life, and death to accept the victories destined for your life with towers flowing over.

4. Sometimes God must remove ashes, and give you beauty.

5. Sometimes God must put you down for you to know what up is and know you are a living miracle.

6. Sometimes God must snatch something from you, so you know what true love is

7. Sometimes God will change the situation in your family so you will appreciate what you have.

8. God will give you strength when you thought you did not have it in you to make a move.

9. God will change situations in your life for the better,

Committed and conceited, walking the mile but in unity. Christ does not just tell us about how He is with us, but He wants us to know that all authority and power are in His hands. Our services are backed with His power. Examine me O Lord.

Let us move forward, a change for the better as a new beginning. Anyone that wants to ride this train better get on board.

I can honestly say I have been blessed. I had to shed some tears and endured some heartaches. I have been in the valley and been in the wilderness but through it, all the Lord has been good to me.

Let us get some prayers answered, ask God to let you know if you are hindering yourself or others around you. Have confidence when you pray. Our Heavenly Father can be trusted to give us gifts that are beneficial in every way.

And once you examine yourself, wait on God's perfect timing. I know something is about to explode.

Think about Mary and Martha, Jesus took his time going to them. Lazarus was dead. And when Jesus went there, He did something better than healing, He raised the dead. God has power over death. No matter what you think is going on or you are going through, nothing is too hard for my God.

Let us examine ourselves and trust what God has for us.

It is revival time. Let us see what God has in store for us.

CHAPTER TWENTY

The Way To Pray

Matthew 6:9-13

It has been a tough year, dealing with all the stress that comes with th pandemic, life, or the news around us. But leaning on the Lord' words always seems to bring us down. So, this is the Lord's praye broken down:

Our Father which art in heaven

This is a personal relationship with our Father in heaven, w recognized that He is our Creator. We talk to Him just like He is ou Father. Addressing Him head-on, and with intimacy.

Hallowed be Thy Name

Because we have intimacy with God, we cannot forget who He is He is Holy, He is righteous, He is King of Kings and Lord of Lords. W should reflect on His holiness and righteousness.

Thy Kingdom Come

Thy will be done, on earth, as it is in heaven. Give it all to The Lord Submit to Him and this helps to look forward to a time of future lessing. You are inviting God to be involved and accomplish whatever He sees necessary in your life and others you pray for. You welcome His rule personally and whole-hearted.

Give us this day our daily bread

You are asking God to provide food for you today whether it is physically or spiritually. And this shows us depending on The Lord is a daily choice. We must trust Him for our physical needs.

And forgive us our debts, as we forgive our debtors

Forgiveness can seem to be the easiest thing to do until you are the one that must forgive. But it is one of the greatest pieces of evidence that you understand the grace God gave you by forgiving you of your sins. Only a forgiven heart can approach God and enjoy His presence.

And lead us not into temptation but deliver us from evil.

God Himself was tempted for forty days in the wilderness. This prepares us for spiritual warfare. And this reminds us that we must depend on Him for strength and enable us to resist temptation. God will not allow us to be tempted beyond what we can handle.

For thine is the power, and the glory, forever. Amen

I give all the glory to my God; He has always shown us that He loves us unconditionally. We honor you with all our heart, thank you for dying on the cross for us. Where would we be if it had not been for you? You give us strength, courage, and love to deal with this untoward generation. We look to You for healing and deliverance and you give it to all for free. All we must do is ask and believe. Lord help us to know you are the Almighty God and that there is none beside you nor before you. Lord, we give our all to you this day. Thank you for taking the stress of life from us and replacing it with peace of mind.

CHAPTER TWENTY-ONE

Voice of God

God will always make a way. It may be costly, but He will always make a way. You have a choice to obey God. Yes, I know I talk a lot about obedience, but you must obey. We must have the courage to do the will of God. Peer pressure can be a problem most of the time because we worry about what the next person is saying. But trust our heavenly Father he will make a way out of no way.

We must make sure that we say no to what we need to say no to and yes to what we need to say yes to. The prize that is offered is based on your answer. If not, you know God will say depart from me, but if you say yes, He will welcome you home. I want to go home and be with my Jesus. So, make sure your offer is from God and not the trick of the enemy. Keep in mind that there are three enemies. As I stated in an earlier chapter: 1-world, 2 Devil and3 flesh. These three must be put under submission and know God will never tell you to do anything wrong, it is not the will of God.

I have to say this, sometimes when we pray, we say God if it is your will when we already know it is not the will of God. We just want to make ourselves feel good and justify our actions. Know God and His voice, listen, and pray. Do not put your convictions down to any sin. When you do this, it gets easier to do every time until you do not feel it nymore. It is worth it to obey God than deal with the consequences that will happen. It is like you sticking your hand in the fire, you get burnt. So, say no to the fire, it comes to steal, kill, and destroy.

If you must walk alone so be it, your reward will be great. I remember in my earlier years when things would go wrong or not my way. It would push me away from the Word of God. Because my thinking was if these people that are supposed to be Christian act like this, I can get the same thing in the world, little did I know I was headed to hell. This walk is not easy, but I will not trade it for anything. I turned toward the world for help and all it got me was pain and suffering. Then one night we were at a conference at the campground, there was a preacher there that said, "If you want anything from the Lord come through the prayer line. "The line was long, but I decided to go get in line. I thought everything I was going through was everybody else's fault. I took no blame for it. When it was my time I was waiting for this big word, looking for sympathy from God or anyone.

The preacher simply placed his hand on my forehead, and these are the exact words he said, "BE OBEDIENT" and removed his hand. I was in shock, I said, "That is all Lord? I am going through right now and that's all I get?"

But I took what he said and started reading scriptures in the Bible on obedience. Prayed hard and started trusting what God said. I was suffocating during this time, it seemed like I had to lift my head over clouds to breathe and catch fresh air. I was like this for some time after. Then one day during the service we had a visiting minister (Bro. Duke). He preached you must dig deep to remove some hurt sometimes. And then he said at the top of your lungs if you are going through something that you just can not shake off, scream to God. Do not stop until you are set free. I remember that day was a change for me. I follow direction and I know that service was ordained by God. I can tell you I have never been the same since. Not only do I walk for my God, but I run for him. He says jump. I say how high. There's nothing that I would change because of this it made me a better person in the Lord.

I do not have the fear of rejection, so trusting my God is a must. Now I can be confident during my storms and knowing that the Lord will come and see about me when I need him the most.

I challenge any of you, know your worth, and do not let anyone change that. I think sometimes I have a little too much confidence because I do not mind working for the Lord and being a laborer for His kingdom. If it had not been for the Lord on my side where would I be?

Now is the time to let God in and if you are going through just be obedient and follow His plan for your life. Thank God I am not what used to be, still striving for perfection in the Lord.

CHAPTER TWENTY-TWO

Overcomer

1 Corinthians 13:12

Anytime someone dies, it is an absolute shock. We say "She died too soon, why did God take her now? And what will we do now?" All these are good questions, but we must realize that the disciples were right there with Jesus and still had questions for him.

But we all know that Jesus makes no mistakes, of course, He is God. Death is a hard thing to go through, I know when my mother transitioned I felt like she took part of me with her. My inside was torn to pieces, I could not even think right. I kept a straight face around people. I hid behind my smile and my clowning around. Some days were harder than others. You have people in your ear telling you, you are a Christian you suppose to have more faith than that. But all that is good but when it comes to death some of us are not that strong, the flesh is weak. And even Jesus Himself, hanging on the cross of Calvary with his armed stretch wide, and his head lifted said, "My God, My God why have You forsaken Me?" But learned that we do not see the world as God sees it and that we must have faith and trust that God knows best and will never make a mistake. That is what it means to walk in faith, and that can be hard when you are in a tough situation.

Praising and praying to God are the tools you use when everything else fails. People can tell you they are praying for you, saying all the right words but until you get to that place of trusting God despite a broken heart, you will never know that peace. I tried Him at His word and leaned on my heavenly father. I tell you; the hurt does not go away but the pain eases up. You begin to look back and laugh at some of the things your loved one has done or reminisce with family. But you must be willing to take the first step and let God do the rest. So, strap on your harness and ride the faith train.

Death is something that we will never understand but I come to realize we are born to die. And one day all of us will go through the same fate. Just be ready when He calls make sure you have accepted the Lord as your Savior and be filled with the baptism of the Holy Ghost and speak in tongues. Acts 2:38, "Then Peter said unto them, Repent, and be baptized every one of you in the name of Jesus Christ for the remission of sins, and ye shall receive the gift of the Holy Ghost."

I thank God for the joy and peace that He has placed in my heart and soul. I can now rejoice and know that He is a loving God and will never put anything on us that we cannot handle. So, death is not a bad thing, it just caught us by surprise, and we must go through our mourning period and then get up in the victory.

I will not tell you that I will not ever cry or be sad about death. I could not say that and be truthful, but I do know that God will give me the strength to go through it with Him by my side.

We will never know the truth about death until we meet our heavenly father, so right now keep the memory of your friend or loved ones.

CHAPTER TWENTY-THREE

Encouraging One Another
Philippians 2:1-8

We need to be more encouraging to one another and stand in the face of opposition so if there is any room for repentance it will be done. We must love one another as Christ loves us and in the presence of the Spirit of God in us, we must know that we are responsible for other souls. If the spirit of God is upon us and dwells within us, we are to encourage one another! I speak to myself sometimes and say, "Faye you need to be an encouragement to your brothers and sister as well as your family. Stay Godly. What would God do if He were in this or that situation?" Hebrews 10:25, "Not forsaking the assembling of ourselves together, as the manner of some is; but exhorting one another: and so much the more, as ye see the day approaching."

My God knows how Christians should encourage each other, so we need to follow God's outline. Assembling shows we are in this together. We fight devils and ungodly spirits together. When we skip being together it makes you feel like you are in it alone all by yourself. God feels like He is a long way off and you cannot reach Him. But when you have your brothers and sisters with you, you will feel like you have that backup. Where three or more are together God is in the mist. With that being said, it is encouraging seeing everyone lifting the name of Jesus, preaching, praising, and singing. Just being in the presence of people that loves God.

Ecclesiastes 4:9-12 "Two are better than one; because they have a good reward for their labor. For if they fall, the one will lift his fellow: but woe to him that is alone when he falleth; for he hath not another to help him up. Again, if two lie together, then they have heat: but how can one be warm alone? And if one prevails against him, two shall withstand him; and a threefold cord is not quickly broken."

Be determined to worship with others for prayer, Bible studies, and any other event that brings you together. Be a part of God's team. Let folk see your devotion and courage, be the light in someone's life. You have so much power that will overflow on others and make them feel like they can make it.

Romans 1:12, "That is, that I may be comforted together with you by the mutual faith both of you and me."

We are not meant to be lived in isolation, we are to work together and encourage others as well as ourselves in the Lord.

Tell others how much you appreciate them, that they look nice today, and speak life into someone. We have been chosen by God and we are born again to living hope through the resurrection of Jesus Christ. We are protected by the power of God. So, we must speak to people about spiritual and godly things. Sometimes you can send a person a notecard, email, text, or phone call just to say I love you in Christ and I was just thinking about you today. Some of us know we have the power, but a little attention helps us just at the right time.

1 Corinthians 14:25 "And thus are the secrets of his heart made manifest, and so falling down on his face he will worship God, and report that God is in you of a truth."

Build up each other and know that God will come when you need Him. Remember the walls of Jericho, everything seemed impossible, but the walls came tumbling down. When you are together nothing is impossible with the Lord on your side. I urge you, encourage the weak or fainthearted, be patient with others. Tell them that God loves them, remind them of the last victory they won, and that God answers prayers. God can handle whatever you have done. There is nothing too hard for God.

Lend a helping hand! Join in the fight! Stand by and with them. Engage in prayer with them, sometimes it is hard to pray when you are sad. But when you have someone there helping you pray it makes a big difference. God is life and we can be the jumper cable. Yes, pray on their behalf. The effective prayer of a righteous man can accomplish much." This is spiritual warfare and prayer is a most effective weapon. Sometimes, the ones you are helping and encouraging don't even have to know, just show them godly love and do the rest.

CHAPTER TWENTY-FOUR

Mercy and Comfort

2 Corinthians 1:3-5

W hen life is tiring, when you are struggling with your sin it is eas to be discouraged and not sure where your comfort is going t come from.

Discouragement is from hell. It steals your joy, your peace, and you zeal.

Be encouraged because God is a God of mercy and comfort. God i called the Father of Mercies. I do not know where I would be if it ha not been for his mercy on me.

He is the author of mercy, which brings salvation, the forgiveness o sin, and deliverance from eternal damnation. Because He shed His bloo for us, I can thank Him for his mercy and comfort. Thank you, Lord, fo being the God of mercy. And do not forget, He will send the Comforte (Holy Ghost). We can receive comfort by faith because God says He the Comforter, then we need to believe that he will provide that comfor when we need it. Also, from others, because a friend or loved one ca give you a comforting word. The Word of God are words o encouragement themselves by the Holy Ghost, which is called th Comforter.

We have afflictions because we live in this fallen world, but this will make you stronger knowing God is on your side. Consider it pure joy whenever you face trials because they will make you better through the comfort and mercy of our Lord. We do not have to think God will not take care of us; he already did when He died on the cross. I am so glad I know He lives. You know being used by God makes you feel good. We need to praise God that we can help other people whether to be physically or spiritually.

Thank you, God, for the gift of encouragement, we do not have to live in a world of hurt and doubt. We do not have to live alone or cry to ourselves. We have the body of Christ to fill us with joy. We have the Word to guide and teach us. And the Holy Ghost that directs our path and lives within us.

We are children of a King, mercy, and comfort will keep us humble knowing our God is a loving God and there is no other God besides Him. He will protect us from our past and future. He will prepare a place for us when we cannot keep ourselves safe.

The Lord that we serve is the King of Kings and the Lord of Lords and I trust Him for the rest of my life. Trusting the Lord will always make your faith stand out. Just hold to His unchangeable hands. He will not leave or forsake you. Mercy and Comfort will guide you through every situation. Just know who you know and that is Jesus Christ our Savior.

You do not have to beg for anything, ask God for it with faith, and believe it is done.

Through this, I believe God is going to do miracles and change lives. I am waiting to see the difference this book makes in someone's life because I know my God always has a ram in the bush for me. I thank him for the favor in my life. I do not take it lightly. I am humble, but I know my God.

CHAPTER TWENTY-FIVE

Obedience

Exodus 19:5

O bedience to God's command is the sign of your love for Him and following what the word of God says. Yes, it requires us to follow Jesus in whichever way His Spirit will lead and direct us. Give all to the Lord, you are not your own. A Disciple is one that can be disciplined.

Everything must come secondary to Jesus. He should be your first love. We cannot allow anything to come between us and the Lord. Meaning attitudes, disobedience, and not doing the will of God.

Let the Word of God be in you so you can overcome the wilds of the wick one. Love one another. Appreciate one another.

Cain was on the ground. The only thing that prevents Cain from doing right was a sin.

The only thing that is keeping some of us from doing right is sin in our lives. Trying to cover up things. The only thing that we are getting away with is being a liar and sinner. It is bad when we have the Holy Ghost and still walk around like we are better than God. God forbids.

Some of us do not have the fear of God, but we better listen, because time is running out. God is coming again. Will we be ready, or will we still hide behind the double-life we are trying to hide?

We are bound by the things of the Word and the way people want us to be. Obedience is prayer, commitment, and trusting God. If we trust God when things get too tough, He will see us through, even if He must send an angel. God will send an angel to rescue you when you are in need.

Instead of throwing in the towel walk through like a soldier of the Lord. You must desire to be like a Christian. When you stop growing in Christ you will die and fade away and start doing things you use to do slowly.

Stop trying to be like someone else, be like Jesus. That is the first step in obedience is to make God your first love and be willing to change to please Him. Walking according to flesh and not the spirit is like a well without water. It is better that you never knew the way of righteousness, than having known it and to turn from the holy commandment delivered to you. It is like a dog returning to his vomit.

People are going to walk in their lust and question God. Like they do not believe His word or His coming. But I am here to tell the same Jesus will return and I do believe it is at hand right now. Now is the time to get together to pray and seek God like never. I do not want to get caught with my work undone. I know God destroyed the world with a flood once, this time it will be with fire.

Be careful because the time will come when people are not going to want to hear sound doctrine and anything else about Christ. They will want a doctrine that's going to satisfy their desires, sit in church listening to the Pastor, leave the church and do the opposite of what the Man of God is speaking on, and not being in the will of God.

We serve a loving God, and He will always take us back no matter what the situation is. I come to you in the name of Jesus Christ, today make a plan to follow Him. Do not let heaven close and you are not ready. Accept Christ today and His ways. You do not know if you will live to see tomorrow. Witness any time, anywhere. Saul has done it in prison at midnight and during a dark and stormy time. Paul did it while the ship he was one sunk.

CHAPTER TWENTY-SIX

Rainbow in the Sky

The rainbow was a covenant God made with Noah when they came out of the ark. Water covered the whole earth, every living thing on it perished. God made a covenant, and to seal His covenant He made a rainbow in the sky for all to see that He is a God that keeps His word. When anyone sees the rainbow, they would know instantly what the sign meant. God is in total control, not us, just Jesus.

Genesis 9:13, "I do set my bow in the cloud, and it shall be for a token of covenant between me and the earth."

He will never destroy the earth by flood. God made a promise and He always keeps His promises. Can you think of someone who always keeps their promises? Someone who would not go back on their promises even if it meant life or death? Let me answer that for you, NO, man cannot take the place of God nor hold His position.

God placed the rainbow in the sky as a symbol of mercy but His mercy will not be extended forever. He said that the earth would be destroyed with fire this time. So, it is important to trust God at His word and take what He says seriously. God's word is stronger than a legal agreement, this is a permanent bond.

No matter how wicked people become, the covenant will last forever. This is a wondrous sign of grace and mercy. Hanging in the sky is a sign of peace, knowing our God is one that keeps His word. This rainbow is a reminder for us, but it is also a reminder for Him. It is not that God has to remember for He is God but that this is a further assurance He will keep His promise. We serve an awesome God.

The rainbow is so beautiful, and the colors are amazing. It appears sometimes after a storm, just like God always coming back and putting some joy in a bad situation.

As a symbol of peace and God's faithfulness to his promises. Yes, He is faithful during or after the storm of trial, we are always assured of the peace of God, which passeth all understanding, which shall keep our hearts and minds through Christ Jesus. But we should remember that God created the rainbow because of sin in the world.

God has a purpose even during a storm. All things work together for our good. The storm will come but God promises us it is for our good.

The next time you look at a rainbow, remember that God knows what He is doing and makes no mistakes.

CHAPTER TWENTY-SEVEN

Holy Ghost

Acts 2:38

Receiving the Holy Ghost is one of the greatest things in this world. The Holy Ghost is better than wine. If you ever want to be high, try Jesus. The Holy Ghost makes you love your enemies. Thank you, God, for the Holy Ghost.

Isaiah 28:11-12," For with stammering lips and another tongue will he speak to this people. To whom he said, This is the rest wherewith ye may cause the weary to rest, and this is the refreshing: yet they would not hear."

Joel 2: 23-29, "Be glad then, ye children of Zion, and rejoice in the Lord your God: for he hath given you the former rain moderately, and he will cause to come down for you the rain, the former rain, and the latter rain in the first month. And the floors shall be full of wheat, and the vats shall overflow with wine and oil. And I will restore to you the years that the locust hath eaten, the cankerworm, and the caterpillar, and the palmerworm, my great army which I sent among you. And ye shall eat in plenty, and be satisfied, and praise the name of the Lord your God, that hath dealt wondrously with you: and my people shall never be ashamed.

And ye shall know that I am in the midst of Israel, and that I am the Lord your God, and none else: and my people shall never be ashamed.

And it shall come to pass afterward, that I will pour out my spirit upon all flesh; and your sons and your daughters shall prophesy, your old men shall dream dreams, your young men shall see visions: And also upon the servants and upon the handmaids in those days will I pour out my spirit."

In the book of Joel, it was foretold what was going to happen. When God gave us the Holy Ghost, He gave it to us according to the word.

God can fill an individual heart with His spirit, but we must have faith. If you do not have faith you will not receive the Holy ghost. Hold on to God and faith, believe, and trust God. Must have faith in God and not in self, to receive the Holy Ghost, believing that you can receive it. Faith by itself is no good, but faith with obeisance brings results.

Matthew 28:19 Go ye, therefore, and teach all nations, baptizing them in the name of the Father, and of the Son, and of the Holy Ghost:

Ingredients to the Name: Jesus is the Name, one name not three. We are not talking about manifestation; we are talking about the name. Father, Son, and the Holy Ghost are one.

Repentance prepares our hearts to obey the scriptures further. And it is turning away from sin to God. First, we must believe on the Lord Jesus to be saved.

Acts 16:31, "Jesus said, "I will not leave you comfortless, I will come to you." The Holy Ghost is Jesus in spirit form!

These three titles: Son, Father, and Holy Ghost has different roles of the same ONE GOD. He is Father in creation; Son in redemption; Holy Ghost in his body, the church!

You do not receive automatically when you believe. It is a separate but dynamic experience that is part of the new birth. Paul found believers, but they needed their experience with God updated! Even though they had been baptized unto John's baptism, it was not enough. They were rebaptized in the name of the Lord Jesus Christ. And the evidence of the Holy Ghost is speaking in tongues. Tongues was the initial or immediate evidence of the Holy Spirit baptism. Acts2:4, 10:45-46, 19:6 all mention tongues as the sign when receiving the Holy Ghost.

Acts 2:39, "For the promise is unto you, and to your children, and to all that are afar off, even as many as the Lord our God shall call."

The power of the Holy Ghost convicts, teaches, equips, and empowers the people of God to grow in grace and spread the gospel to the nations for the glory of God.

Without communicating with God, you will find yourself lonely.

God is good and He is faithful to perform His word. I am trusting God for the Holy Ghost.

The promise is ours, so receive it today.

"God is a Spirit: and they that worship him must worship Him in spirit and in truth." John 4:24

"Jesus said, "But ye shall receive power after that the Holy Ghost is come upon you." Act 1:8

CHAPTER TWENTY-EIGHT

You are Blessed

Psalms 118:17-18, "I shall not die, but live, and declare the works of the Lord. The Lord hath chastened me sore: but he hath not given me over unto death."

During life, we end up in places we never thought we would be mentally, physically, emotionally, materially, spiritually. We visioned that life had more for us, and this could not be happening to me. We have high hopes and dreams. We visioned that our spouses and children would be the model Christians that you asked God for, that our paychecks would be bigger, life would just be grand. But as we look around our reality, it has not gone as we planned, and our dreams have been scattered.

We cry and we pray but never really get it in our spirit that if God said it, then it will get better. Then we adjust our dreams to go with everyday life for today and stop pushing for more, thinking that it is better to just accept the status of our situation. We quit in the middle when we are next in line for a miracle.

But I am here to tell you, do not throw the towel in right now. It may appear that all hope is gone, that everyone else is finishing the race without you and being blessed with things, family and spiritually, God said it is not over yet. Put in your spirit that I shall not die, I shall not quit, I shall not give up but instead, I will live and survive because I serve a prayer-answering God. There will be mountains, valleys, some hard times, some tests, and tribulations, but during all of that, you will still have God on your side. David went through some of the same things, but he had an anointing on his life. Could it be that we can have that same anointing on our life if we just hold on and trust God at His word?

We are going to go through trials and may feel defeated, but David found himself wrestling a bear and lion and was able to kill them. There are no circumstances that we face that are going to defeat us if we face our giants.

God will speak promises over our lives, there is no weapon formed against us that could truly prosper. There is no battle we cannot win because God is a very present help in the time of trouble and yea though enemies should rise up against us they shall stumble and fall because in the time of trouble God will hide us in the shelter of his tabernacle. Weeping will only endure for a night because my God will bring joy in the morning.

Our testimony comes from our experiences going through with God in our life, not that life has always been easy but the Love of a Father, our God. The testimony comes because of the testing. Life will bring some difficult times no matter how saved and sanctified we may be there is no way around the arrows of this thing called life. It seems like the more you do the right thing the harder the storms come against you. We know that temptations are most of the time put there so we can fail. The temper himself comes to steal, kill, and destroy. So, when you become an overcomer thank God for your testimony. God's desire is not for us to fail and the word says that God will not tempt us. This is the devil's trap. Trials are like being in a courthouse, innocent until proven guilty.

God's desire for us to stand blameless before Him He will not send trials our way for us to fail, He said He will never put anything on us that we cannot handle.

We are being put through a test and test is what God sends our way to prepare us for our testimony so count it all joy when you are going through knowing that you will see light in the tunnel very soon. Testing is for our good because it is in the testing that God can purge us, reshape us, mold us, and transform us into what it is He needs us to be. There is a blessing on the other side if we just go through the test. The pain and suffering that we go through now is just the icing on the cake and it all has a purpose. There is nothing in life that does not have a purpose. We must find our purpose with God. I heard someone say there is a reason for the madness. Let us thank God for the madness so we can unwrap the goodness of Christ Jesus.

God has mercy on us when we fail a test, He allows us to take it over, and over again until we pass the test. What a merciful God we serve. After we pass, we can move on to the next level of trials and tests. We serve a God where the impossible is possible.

Understand that every time you allow anything, anyone to turn you away from what Christ has for you, you have given the adversary victory. We have to learn to trust God, even when we are going through the storm God will help us to know that all things work together for the good of those that are called according to His purpose. And that God is a very present help in the time of trouble. Then you can step in this thing that is called life and won't sink because He will never leave nor forsake us. Everything in or around us must be still. The storm will be peaceful and you will be able to walk on water.

The main thing is to intercede in prayer for our loved ones and calling the things that are not as though they were. I shall not die, but live and declare the work of the Lord.

Intercessory prayer is not the same as a prayer for yourself, it is putting someone else's needs before your own and believing that God will move in that situation. God is our lawyer in a courtroom, and He will always stand up for us in our time of need. In our intercessory prayers for others, we can only stand in the gap between Satan and their destruction. We are not God so we cannot atone for their sin but pray for their soul and stand in the gap for them. The word says the effectual fervent prayer of a righteous man availed much. God has the last word; all we must do is pray and believe what we asked Him for.

Saints, life gets hard sometimes, but we must strive for perfection and keep loving God and know that it is not over yet. We shall live and not die; we speak life over our loved ones and ourselves in the mighty name of Jesus.

ABOUT THE AUTHOR

Faye Thomas grew up in Social Circle, Ga. She loves her family. God put writing a book in her spirit and now there will be more to come. Faye has been married to John K. Thomas for 3 years. She has three children and five grandchildren.

She is the HR Manager/Administrator of five facilities and believes that patients' care should be a manager's first priority. Her first love is to serve the Lord with humility

Fay Thomas is available for
Training, Conferences, or Sermons.
Please contact her booking agent:

Attention:
Faye Thomas Ministries
Blessings@fayethomasministries.com
fayethomas2@yahoo.com
(678) 227-4881